Scripture-Based Liturgies

Ian Tarrant

Senior Anglican Chaplain, University of Nottingham

GROVE BOOKS LIMITED
RIDLEY HALL RD CAMBRIDGE CB3 9HU

Contents

Thanks

People too many to name have helped with the preparation of this booklet, but I would like to record special thanks to Colin Buchanan, Carolyn Headley and Jenny Petersen for contributing liturgies, and to Trevor Lloyd and Anna de Lange for commenting on the whole booklet as it was being put together. The Scripture quotations in the Hebrews liturgy are from The New Revised Standard Version of the Bible, Anglicized Edition, © 1989, 1995 by the Division of Christian Education of the National Council of the Churches of Christ in the United States of America, and are used by permission. All rights reserved.

The Cover Illustration is by Peter Ashton

First Impression April 2003
ISSN 0144-1728
ISBN 1 85174 527 0

Liturgy in Scripture and Vice Versa

This booklet presents a handful of liturgies which are strongly based on a particular Scripture passage or book of the Bible.

They are not intended for regular use, but might be useful in particular one-off contexts such as a church away-day, or to introduce a sermon or housegroup series. In addition, you could take up the ideas to produce similar liturgies for your own situation.

In the many forms of writing in the Bible, we encounter words of worship in different ways—quoted in narrative and in letters, and sometimes presented with little guide as to the original context. On the other hand, the worship of God's people, in temple and synagogue, home and church, has often drawn on the words of Scripture, to inform and to inspire, to pray and to praise. Here are just a few examples of the interplay between liturgy and Scripture:

- The original use of the Psalms in the worship of Israel has been discussed by scholars such as Mowinckel and Gunkel. Were certain psalms used for specific festivals, or at particular points in the worship? Were they sung by the congregation or by a choir? Nevertheless the early church adopted the Psalms for Christian worship, and in many churches psalms are still used—said, chanted, or sung, but perhaps not as the original writers intended.

- When David had amassed the materials for the building of the temple, 'he praised the LORD in the presence of the whole assembly' using words recorded in detail in 1 Chronicles 29.10–19. His words, abbreviated and paraphrased, have been used in Christian churches, and appear as the first of the *Prayers at the Preparation of the Table* in *Common Worship*[1].

- The only passage where Paul writes in detail of the earthly life of Jesus is his account of the institution of Holy Communion, 1 Corinthians 11.23–25. We assume that this story was a part of the liturgical tradition of the earliest church which became embedded in Paul's teaching, and of course is part of modern liturgical tradition as well.

- Philippians 2.6–11 is presumed to be an early Christian hymn or creed which Paul quotes as he calls for unity and humility amongst the Christians in Philippi. In *Common Worship* it becomes an *Authorized Affirmation of Faith*[2].

- It has been argued that the whole of 1 Peter is an Easter baptismal liturgy, later edited into letter form.[3] I have yet to find evidence of anybody editing it back into a service!

- Alan Garrow suggests that the book of Revelation is comprised of six texts, each one originally used in a liturgical context.[4] Many short passages from Revelation are used in contemporary liturgy; but Alan has 'conducted a number of eucharists using the second instalment (4.1–7.19) at study days around the country.'[5]

Paul encourages the Christians at Colossae to 'Let the word of Christ dwell in you richly as you teach and admonish one another with all wisdom, and as you sing psalms, hymns and spiritual songs with gratitude in your hearts to God' (Colossians 3.16). Believing that all Scripture is God-breathed, we look for different ways to apprehend and comprehend God's words:

- **reading** the Bible quietly for oneself.
- **hearing** it read out loud by somebody else.
- **seeing** it acted—professionally produced films and plays are great, but you can do it yourself in church too. One resource for this is the *Dramatised Bible*[6] but there are numerous others.[7] Consider also the possibility of dramatised reading which needs less space and less skill, or having people mime the actions while one person reads the text. (Of course the actors themselves are not only seeing and hearing the text, but **doing** it as well!)
- **singing** the Scriptures in hymns, songs, choruses, chants.
- **praying** it in well-crafted prayers or responses[8]—much of our liturgy is redrafted Scripture.

These different encounters with the Bible touch us in different ways—informing us, moving us, transforming us, reaching different parts of our minds and hearts.[9]

The services in this booklet are opportunities for getting more deeply involved with a book or passage of Scripture. Some are based on a narrative —here the worshipper enters into the plot stage by stage, identifying with the characters. Some are based on letters—here the worshipper encounters more of the text (in different forms) than they would comfortably read at a single sitting.

A Variety of Approaches 2

In his book, An Earthful of Glory, Philip Newell offers twenty-one complete services, each of which draws on a particular biblical author or book.[10]

He has both a Morning Prayer and an Evening Prayer for each of the seven books: Isaiah, Wisdom, Job, Jeremiah, Ecclesiasticus, Hosea and Song of Songs. These could easily be used in a Church of England Service of the Word. In each case he provides:

- an opening sentence from the book
- an opening prayer, typically of 15 short lines, based on ideas in the book
- two canticles, of which at least one is taken from the named book, though the other may come from elsewhere in Scripture
- prayers of thanksgiving and intercession, typically 20 lines, again drawing on the chosen book
- a closing prayer, typically of 10 lines.

However, the Holy Communion services he provides are less useful for Anglicans. Again there are seven, one each based on John the Evangelist, Peter, Paul, James the Just, Luke, Hebrews and Revelation. Within an unchanging structure, the elements that draw on the chosen book are:

- an opening sentence
- the eucharistic prayer
- a closing prayer

He suggests that all this material might be used on a weekly cycle—the readings being those set by one's lectionary, not related to the liturgy of the day. The liturgies in this booklet differ from Newell's work in that they are designed as one-off services, complete in themselves, not to be used with a lectionary. And for all but the last, the structure of the liturgy parallels the structure of the Bible passage. Newell's work may not be appropriate for every context, but it shows what can be done in the creative use of biblical texts within the setting of worship.

Having a Go

Newell's approach or the examples in this booklet might whet your appetite for more: why not try to write your own? Here are some suggestions as to how you might approach the task, on your own or with others in the congregation responsible for worship, praying that God's Spirit will help you 'get inside' the text.

1 *Choose your text.* Not every passage of Scripture can be treated this way! Look for a structure which can be mirrored in your service. Obviously a story about an encounter can map onto a service structure like this:

Narrative	Liturgy
A meets B	The gathering
A & B interact	Teaching/prayer/sacrament
A & B separate	The dismissal

Different and more complex structures are also possible!

2 *Consider how you will handle different parts of the text.* These are just some of the options open to you:

- Reading or drama
- Versicle and response between leader and people, left and right sides of the church, adults and children...
- Song
- Action—walking (in procession?), sharing food (Communion?), washing (of feet?), greeting (the Peace?), dance...
- Prayer

3 *Consider the learning that will take place.* How will this be facilitated—by a sermon, by study in groups, silence, or something else?

4 *Look at the overall balance, and adjust if necessary.* Is there too much or too little of something? Do you need to draw on another passage?[11] Are you complying with whatever liturgical regulations pertain?[12] Will your congregation be taken somewhere new—and not *too* far out of their 'comfort zone'?

You may make some false starts as you try with different texts—do not be disheartened, but persevere until something clicks![13]

Scripture Journeys

Some churches have a tradition of involving the people in the story of Easter through the Stations of the Cross, walking a route inside or outside a church building, with a number of stopping points. At each station there is an image of an event in the story, the appropriate verses are read, and there can be reflection, prayer or singing. The stations can be permanent architectural features or set up temporarily. It is possible to base similar Scripture journeys on other narratives (perhaps a parable or the life of a prophet), with a text and prayer suggestions at each station. Individuals or small groups can set off on the journey at different times, and move along the route at their own pace.[14]

Drama and Worship Interwoven

A home group of a west London church was asked to lead an evening service based on the letter to Philemon. After studying the letter, they decided to invite the congregation to join in the worship of the first-century church in Colossae...

> The home group members sat on cushions in a circle on the floor, the other twenty people sat on chairs in a larger concentric circle. The home group led the worship, as the Colossians might have worshipped, with a service much like Evening Prayer: an opening chorus, a confession, a canticle, a Psalm, and a reading from the Old Testament. Then (surprise!) a messenger from Paul the Apostle arrived, bearing a letter for Philemon, one of the Colossian congregation. 'Philemon' read the letter out loud to the congregation, the messenger brought in 'Onesimus' who had been waiting in the shadows, and a drama unfolded, as the elders of Colossae convinced Philemon that he should be reconciled to his former slave...making due reference, of course, to the letter received.
>
> Once the matter had been settled, worship continued, with songs of praise, prayers for captives and refugees, the Lord's Prayer, a collect, and the grace.

A good deal of care was needed in the planning and presentation, so that although worship and drama were interwoven, the worship was always genuine, and appropriate for both the first century and the present century. The drama provided a setting for the reading of the letter, and an exposition of its significance. Those who had been involved in the planning, and those who had not, found the whole service meaningful and memorable.[15]

3   The Scripture-based Liturgies

The five examples which follow have come from a variety of authors, who prepared their liturgies for distinct contexts.

While we have attempted to make the texts conform to certain typographic norms, the degree of detail and commentary in the texts varies. Draw what you can from each example—and be encouraged and inspired to encounter the Scriptures anew!

Luke 24—An Ecumenical Easter Communion Service

Introduction

Occasion: An ecumenical service for Oxford colleges and courses involved in theological education. A working group representing all the different participants produced the service.[16]

Theme: The walk on the Emmaus Road, and a celebration of the new life and the new start of the resurrection.

Shape: A one hour service, followed by a meal together.

The service uses the story of the Road to Emmaus to give a sense of journeying together as we recognize Jesus with us.

As we clearly celebrate Easter as those who *know* he is risen, rather than being in the confusion and sadness of the two on the road, the service does not follow the story exactly. It does however provide us with a general shape that is reflected in the various elements of service—as the outline shows.

The service and meal are seen as integral—so that we have a sense of Jesus' presence with us as we 'break bread together' at the meal. The service sheet explains this, and explains that for this reason the order of service does not exactly fit the story at this point.

The service ends with the sense that all the disciples are coming together in their excitement that they have seen Christ, and that he has made himself known to them in different ways—thus celebrating our diversity.

Opening action:

Background music as people come in, then lights off and silence.

Unaccompanied anthem of the story of the Road to Emmaus, during which two 'disciples' walk in together—lighting candles down central aisle as they go, co-ordinated to reach the front at climax of the anthem, then lights on.

The two 'disciples' read 24.13–15a, then step to either side of sanctuary.

Introduction in Service Sheet

In the first days after the resurrection there was a growing sense of excitement and wonder as the disciples met with the risen Lord. Jesus met with them in different places, and made himself known to them in different ways.

This evening we celebrate a common faith, yet find that we too have come to recognize the risen Lord in different ways and through different experiences.

The story of the disciples on the Road to Emmaus, as told in Luke 24, records the process of discovery for two disciples, and their desire to tell the news to others.

The story begins with their confusion at what has happened, and their experience of walking with Christ while yet unable to recognize him; then the sense of excitement as, still unrecognized, he opens up their understanding of the Scriptures and the words of the prophets; then the moment of recognition as Jesus broke bread and they ate together; ending with the dash back to Jerusalem to add their story to the others that gave testimony to the resurrection.

This story shapes our celebration today. It holds some parallels for us, although we have the benefit of all of Scripture and the hindsight of the collective faith of the church over the centuries.

We hope that the quotations from Luke 24 will help us to focus on different aspects of our journey of faith: our realization that Christ is present with us, and yet the recognition that we too have times of confusion or times when his presence is cloaked by lack of understanding or sin; the Creed as a rehearsal of all that we have come to understand as Truth through Scripture and the collective faith of the church, yet still mindful that we do not yet fully understand; the ministry of the Word celebrating the way in which Scripture brings us to greater understanding and the way our hearts are warmed as Christ reveals the Truth through it; prayer as we invite Christ more into every aspect of our lives, our learning, our discipleship and ministry and our world; and a celebration of our faith as we recount some of the many different ways in which God has revealed himself to us.

For the disciples going to Emmaus Jesus made himself known in the breaking of bread as they ate together. So we see the meal together as part of the service. Our fellowship together will continue to celebrate the unity we have in Christ, and will be an opportunity for Christ to be made more fully known to us in one another.

Gathering

Anthem—sung by choir As we walked home at close of day *(J Bell & G Maule)*
Reading   Luke 24.13–15a
Hymn   Jesus calls us here to meet him *(J Bell & G Maule)*
             first 3 verses only; expressing our coming together in God's presence, as the disciples met with Jesus on the Road

Penitence

Reading   Luke 24.15–16

These disciples were kept from recognizing Jesus.

Let us now come in prayer to ask God's forgiveness and mercy for the times when it is we who are at fault, and turn a blind eye to his presence among us.

Let us pray.

Lord Jesus Christ,

We confess that there are times when we have turned against you, when you have become hidden from us by our own sins, when we have chosen to turn away from you and your ways.

For these times when we have rejected you, we are truly sorry:
Lord have mercy.

We confess that there are times when we have failed to recognize your presence in others who are sharing the journey of life alongside us, and failed to show love to them as we would want to show our love to you.

For these times when we have rejected you, we are truly sorry:
Lord have mercy.

We confess that there are times when in our weakness or negligence, we have failed to turn to you in our needs, and have accused you of lack of love for us.

For these times when we have rejected you, we are truly sorry:
Lord have mercy.

We confess that there are times when we have failed to recognize your presence in one another, and have marred the unity of your body by prejudice, misunderstanding, and arrogant judgement.

For these times when we have rejected you, we are truly sorry:
Lord have mercy.

Lord, for all those times when our own choices, desires, sins, and lack of love have blotted you out of our thoughts, words and deeds, we are truly sorry:
Lord have mercy.

In your mercy renew in us such a sense of your presence with us, and such assurance of your promise to us that you are with us to the end of the age— that our whole lives may be lived in the light of the knowledge that you walk beside us.

Lord in your mercy
hear our prayer. Amen.

Song—Cantor and response: Remember, remember your mercy, Lord
(Paul Inwood)

Affirmation of Faith

Reading   Luke 24.17–24

Apostles' Creed in question and response form, as a recitation of the facts as we have received them, echoing the account of what the two disciples rehearsed with Jesus along the way (Common Worship p 143).

Hymn   We have a gospel to proclaim *expressing our belief—a hymn which reflects the record of Christ's passion and resurrection.*

Reading   Luke 24.25–27,32

Song   Open our eyes, Lord, we want to see Jesus

Reading   Isaiah 53.4–12

Sermon	*reflecting vv 25–27 and v 32 when Jesus explained to them what was said in all the Scriptures concerning himself, and they asked themselves—'were not our hearts burning within us' when Jesus talked to them and opened up the Scriptures.*

Reading   Luke 24.28–29

Prayer   *expressing v 29, inviting Jesus to come in to stay with the disciples.*

Intercession

Prayer for unity by greater recognition of Christ in each other.
Prayer for discipleship and ministry—for help in enabling us to recognize Jesus alongside.
Lord's Prayer *expressing our closeness as we recognize Jesus with us.*

Song   Breathe on me, breath of God *(E Hatch) also expressing v 29—a prayer for God to be with us and in us.*

Celebration of faith

Reading   Luke 24.30–31, 33–35

A 'fanfare' of short sentences, in celebration of the different ways in which Jesus has made himself known to us his disciples; concluding with the Easter Acclamation:

Alleluia! Christ is risen.
He is risen indeed. Alleluia!

Hymn   Thine be the glory, risen, conquering Son *expressing joy in faith*

Prayer and Dismissal for meal together, with a repeat of the Easter Acclamation:

Alleluia! Christ is risen.
He is risen indeed. Alleluia!

Before the meal:

Reading   Luke 24.30–31a
The Peace
Thanksgiving for the meal

John 6—A Liturgy for Holy Communion

Introduction

This draft liturgy[17] treats the first half of John chapter 6 as the ministry of the word, composed of narrative with an approximation to original responses. If any variation is desired, then the OT reading about the manna (Exodus 16) could be introduced.

There is no place indicated for a distinct sermon or homily, though it would be easy to introduce that, either after the most appropriate short reading at 1, 3, 5, or 7, or after 8, making the creed the response.

No forms of intercessions are suggested here. Intercessions could take any form usual for intercessions, or, to be true to the tightness of the liturgical dependence upon John 6, could have a sacramental framework. In this case sections of the intercessions would begin from the scriptural text, such as:

> 'Jesus fed the 5000 who were hungry. We pray for those facing famine today.'

> 'Jesus did not want to be made king by force. We pray for those tempted to use violent means for political ends.'

> 'Jesus said he had come to feed our inner selves. We pray for those whose lives are empty within.'

> 'Jesus said he would raise us up at the last day. We remember with gratitude the faithful departed and look forward to being raised with them at that last day.'

The sacramental part of the rite is as tightly drawn from the text of John 6 as the ministry of the word is. This means that in the eucharistic prayer features to which we are accustomed (or which we think almost essential) such as the presence of a narrative of institution or an explicit affirmation that the death of Jesus was the one perfect sacrifice for the sins of the world, have not been intruded into a text which follows the one passage of Scripture. These needs are acknowledged and so have been met allusively—almost *en passant*—within the John 6 development. But the weight in John 6 is on eating and drinking, with little attempt to spell out—either for Jesus' hearers at the time, or for John's first readers—what eating Christ's flesh and drinking his blood actually meant. Obviously, therefore, the rite is so weighted as to be useful (indeed, we hope, inspiring and nourishing) on 'once-off' occasions, but could not be suggested as a regular Sunday liturgy—quite apart from its not meeting the Church of England requirement for an authorized creed or eucharistic prayer.

One compromise suggestion made within our Group was that the John 6 passage should contribute an 'extended preface' to go within an existing authorized eucharistic prayer. Although using such a eucharistic prayer would import extraneous liturgical material into the rite, the suggestion has been met here by an appendix.

No hymnody is provided, nor place for it suggested. The mood of the liturgy is both reflective and repetitive within what is overtly a narrow theme. Thus hymns which introduced unrelated topics could complicate the flow. Obviously, sacramental hymns may have a place, such as

> I am the bread of life
> I hunger and I thirst
> Eat this bread; drink this cup

Or suitable hymns could be used to begin and end the service.

1. *Reading* 6.1–13

2. Have you seen what he has done?
   He has fed five thousand.
   Who then can this man be?
   He must be the prophet to come into the world.

3. *Reading* 6.15–21

4. What has he done upon the lake?
   He has walked on the water and come to the boat.
   And what did he say to you out on the lake?
   He said 'It is I; do not be afraid!'
   Who then can this man be?
   He is the Lord of the lake and the storm!

5. *Reading* 6.22–24

6. What did the crowd say when they found him?
   They said to him 'Rabbi, when did you come here?'
   And what did he tell them they really were seeking?
   Not signs for the eyes, but contentment inside.
   What did he offer in place of food that can perish?
   Food that sustains our eternal life.

7. *Reading* 6.28–31

8. Let us pray.
   Heavenly Father, of old the manna in the wilderness fed your people, giving them strength, but not life eternal;

today, recognizing your Son as the true bread from heaven,
may we feed on him, the life of the world.
We would feed on this bread always.
Give us the bread of life that we may never hunger;
let us drink of Christ that we may never thirst;
Father, let all whom you have given to Christ now draw near to him.
Lord, we believe you will not turn us away.

9. *Affirmation of faith*
We believe in Jesus Christ, God's true bread from heaven;
he came down to earth not to do his own will,
but the will of him who sent him.
This is the will of the Father who sent him,
that he should lose none of those whom the Father gave him,
but should raise them up on the last day.
For this is the Father's will,
that all who look to the Son and believe in him
should have eternal life,
and the Son will raise them up on the last day.

10. *Question and answer (said antiphonally right and left sides)*
R   But was not Jesus born of an earthly mother?
L   **Yes, but he is still the true bread from heaven.**
R   Can he indeed be from heaven and be yet one of us?
L   **Yes, and the Father who sent him draws us to know him.**
R   But surely we have never seen the Father?
L   **No, but we are drawn by him to come to the Son.**
R   Has only the Son then seen the Father?
L   **Yes, and those who believe in him have eternal life.**

11. *Intercessions*

12. *The Peace*
As five thousand shared the bread of one boy
So we would share the bread and wine of our Lord.
The peace of the Lord be shared among you:
and also with you.
Greet each other as sharers in God's feast.

13. *The Preparation of the Table*
Jesus is the bread of life, not to nourish our bodies as ordinary bread, nor
even as the manna which the people of old ate in the desert; no, he is the
bread of life who has come down from heaven, that we should feed on
him and never die.

14. *Eucharistic Prayer*

The Lord is here.
His Spirit is with us.
Lift up your hearts.
We lift them to the Lord.
Let us give thanks to the Lord our God.
It is right to give thanks and praise.
We give you thanks and praise, living Father,
for sending to us Jesus Christ your Son our Lord.
For he is the living bread come down from heaven,
that whoever feeds on him should live forever.
He gave himself for the life of the world
and the bread that he gives is his flesh;
that whoever eats his flesh and drinks his blood
should have eternal life and be raised up by him on the last day.
So, Father, we pray that this bread and this wine
may be to us the true food of his flesh and true drink of his blood,
and that we may abide in him and he in us.

As our Lord fed five thousand with the loaves and fishes,
and taught his disciples to hunger after the bread which truly satisfies,
so, mindful also of his Last Supper with his disciples,
and following his example and obeying his command,
we bless you for this bread and wine of eternal life
that, eating and drinking in accordance with his promise,
we today may also be partakers of his most blessed flesh and blood.

Jesus is the bread who has come down from heaven;
whoever eats this bread will live forever.
He has ascended where he was before,
he has given us his Holy Spirit.
May the Spirit give us his true life;
let our hunger not be met by lesser food.

And so, Father, led by his Spirit, we praise you through him;
his words to us are Spirit and life.
We cannot go to anyone else,
for he has the words of eternal life.
We come to him because you have drawn us;
we praise you through him because he now feeds us.
To you be all praise and glory through him
now and forever.
Amen.

15. *The Lord's Prayer*

16. *Breaking the bread*
Jesus is the bread of God which comes down from heaven.
Lord, give us this bread always.

17. *Invitation and distribution*
Jesus said: 'Those who eat my flesh and drink my blood have eternal life, and I will raise them up on the last day.' Come, eat and drink as he has commanded, and have eternal life as he has promised.

Words of distribution:
The flesh of Christ. R. **The true food**
The blood of Christ. R. **The true drink**

18. *Post-communion*
Jesus says, 'Do you wish to go away from me?'
Lord, to whom could we go? You have the words of eternal life.
He asks, 'Do you then believe?'
Lord, we believe and know that you are the Holy One of God.
Will you then stay with him?
That is our prayer.
Then let us pray.

Living Father, we thank you for feeding us
with the flesh and blood of Jesus Christ your Son,
that we might remain in him, and he in us.
Let your Spirit keep us faithful to him,
that we may live for him in this life
and that he may raise us up at the last day.
For he is the living bread
in whom all our hungers are satisfied.
We praise you through him forever. Amen.

19. *Blessing*
May Jesus the true bread from heaven
feed you all the days of your life
and raise you up at the last day.
And the blessing of God Almighty,
the living Father, the Son who was sent by him,
and the Spirit who gives life,
live within you now and forever.
Amen.

20. *Dismissal*

Go and do the will of the Father:
Not our will but his.
Go in peace, for the Lord has fed you.
Thanks be to God.

Appendix:

The Eucharistic Prayer from John 6.51–65 in the main rite above rendered instead as an 'Extended Preface' for use with Common Worship *Eucharistic Prayers A, B and E*

We give you thanks and praise, living Father,
for sending to us Jesus Christ your Son our Lord.
For he is the living bread come down from heaven,
that whoever feeds on him should live forever.
He gave himself for the life of the world.
and the bread that he gives is his flesh;
that whoever eats his flesh and drinks his blood
should have eternal life and be raised up by him on the last day.
His flesh is food indeed and his blood is drink indeed,
so that, as we eat his flesh and drink his blood,
we abide in him and he in us.
Jesus is the bread who has come down from heaven;
and whoever eats this bread will live forever.
He has ascended where he was before,
and has given us his Holy Spirit.
It is his Spirit who gives us life
and we come to Christ, Father, because you have drawn us.
Therefore with angels and archangels...

Acts 8—A Service of the Word with Affirmation of Baptismal Vows

> **Introduction**
> This service follows the encounter of Philip with the Ethiopian official, and the latter's baptism. The opening versicles and responses, and the baptismal material are taken from *Common Worship*. Most of the other versicles draw on Isaiah, the book that the Ethiopian was reading.
>
> When printing a service sheet, it would be helpful to include the texts of the readings. Minimal music is suggested here—there is scope for much more.

The Gathering

Blessed be God, Father, Son and Holy Spirit.
Blessed be his kingdom, now and for ever. Amen.
There is one body and one Spirit.
There is one hope to which we were called;
one Lord, one faith, one baptism,
one God and Father of all.

Introduction to the service

Reading: Acts 8.26–29

Lord, you have shown us what is good:
to act justly, love mercy, and walk humbly with you.
You call us from every family under heaven
and we meet in the name of your Son.
You have made known your salvation,
and reveal your justice in the sight of the nations.
May your ways be known on the earth,
your saving power among the nations.

The Ministry of the Word

Song: Laudate Dominum *(Taizé)*

Reading: Acts 8.29–34

Reflection on the reading

The Commitment

Reading: Acts 8.35–38

Silence

In baptism, God calls us out of darkness into his marvellous light.
As we recall the baptism of the Ethiopian on the Gaza road, let us each remember also our own baptism, and declare afresh our allegiance to Christ:

*The leader asks the people the six questions of the baptismal decision (Common
Worship p 150) beginning:*

Do you reject...?

*The Alternative Profession of Faith (Common Worship p 373) may then be used,
beginning:*

Let us affirm our common faith in Jesus Christ.

Do you believe and trust...?

The congregation is sprinkled with water
May God cleanse us and renew his life within us
that we may confess his name this day and for ever.
Amen.

The Prayers

The Lord's Prayer is said.

We continue in prayer for the church and the world, using the response:
Your will be done on earth, O Lord *(South African tune: Mayenziwe)*

The prayers conclude with the collect for Epiphany.

The Sending Out

Reading: Acts 8.39–40

As the rain and the snow come down from heaven and water the earth
so does the word of the Lord accomplish his will.
He summons those whom we do not know
and appoints us to be his witnesses.
We shall go out with joy
and be led forth in peace.

The people depart singing.

Philippians—An Office[18]

Introduction

It is the personal element in Philippians which gives it a context—it appears to be a first report from imprisonment in Rome (mentioned at the end of Acts of Apostles). The Philippians have sent a gift of money by Epaphroditus (2.25–30), even though suffering themselves. Paul is sending a letter back by Epaphroditus, thanking them for the money (4.14–19), and expressing his love for them generally—and thus both reporting himself and encouraging them. He hopes to send Timothy to them soon after Epaphroditus has returned (2.19–24).

It looks as if the Philippians got word Paul was on the way to Rome in the Autumn of 59 or 60 AD, when in fact, although he had started, he had been shipwrecked and was spending the winter on Malta (Acts 27–28). Epaphroditus set out with the money, fell ill on the way (and a report went back to Philippi), and then recovered and reached Rome about the same time as Paul.

Philippians is not only encouraging generally—it is almost entirely without rebuke, correction, or reproof from Paul (save only for the two arguing women, 4.2–4), which makes it unique in the Pauline letters.

The possibility of indigestion arises. The office should be taken in a measured, meditative, unhurried way, with time for reflection afterwards.

Grace to you and peace from God our Father and the Lord Jesus Christ.

Pause

In every prayer of mine for you I make my prayers with joy.
We are partners in the gospel from the first day until now.
He who has begun a good work in you
Will carry it to completion until the day of Christ.
It is my prayer that your love may abound more and more,
That we may approve what is excellent
and may be pure and blameless for the day of Christ,
filled with the fruits of righteousness
which come through Jesus Christ,
to the glory and praise of God.

Reading: Philippians 1.12–18

Silence for reflection

For me to live is Christ,
and to die is gain.
I am hard pressed between the two.
my desire is to depart and be with Christ,
But to remain in the flesh is more necessary
for others' progress and joy in the faith.

Let us pray.

Almighty God,
as you have granted to us
that we should not only believe in Christ,
but also suffer for his sake,
may our manner of life be worthy of the gospel
that we may stand firm in one spirit,
with one mind striving for the faith of the gospel,
and without fear of any opponents.
We ask this that it may be a sign of our salvation
through Jesus Christ our Lord.
Amen.

Reading: Philippians 2.1–5

'The Song of Christ's Glory' (said antiphonally: left and right, by half verses):

> Christ Jesus was in the form of God:
>> but he did not cling to equality with God
> He emptied himself taking the form of a servant:
>> and was born in the likeness of men.
> Being found in human form he humbled himself:
>> and became obedient unto death, even death on a cross.
> Therefore God has highly exalted him:
>> and bestowed on him the name above every name,
> that at the name of Jesus every knee should bow:
>> in heaven and on earth and under the earth;
> and every tongue confess that Jesus Christ is Lord:
>> to the glory of God the Father.
> **Glory to the Father and to the Son and to the Holy Spirit**
>> **as it was in the beginning is now and shall be for ever. Amen.**

Work out your own salvation with fear and trembling
for God is at work in us, both to will and to work for his pleasure.
Do everything without complaining or arguing
being blameless and pure as children of God.

Hold out to others the word of life
so that it was not for nothing that others laboured to teach us.
I am glad and rejoice with you all.
We too are glad and rejoice with you.

Let us pray
Prayers based on Philippians 3.1–11

Group Bible Study from Philippians 3.12–21. Groups of three or four have around five minutes to look at the passage, and then each in the group tells the others briefly which verse most strikes him or her and why.

Exhortation from Philippians 4:
Stand firm in the Lord, beloved.

Rejoice in the Lord always; again I will say, 'Rejoice.' Have no anxiety about anything, but in everything by prayer and supplication with thanksgiving let your requests be made known to God.

Finally, my brothers and sisters, whatever is true, whatever is honourable, whatever is just, whatever is pure, whatever is lovely, whatever is gracious, if there is any excellence, if there is anything worthy of praise, think about these things.

Silence

I have learned, in whatever state I am,
therewith to be content.
I know how to be abased,
and I know how to abound.
I have learned the secret of facing plenty and hunger, abundance and want.
I can do all things in him who strengthens me.
My God will supply all your needs through his riches in glory in Christ Jesus.
To our God and Father be glory for ever and ever. Amen.
The peace of God, which passes all understanding, will keep your hearts and minds in Christ Jesus.
The grace of the Lord Jesus Christ be with your spirit.

Hebrews—Morning Prayer[19]

Leader: Today we'll be using a new and different form of Morning Prayer,
based on the old and familiar Letter to the Hebrews.
Because so much of this service is taken straight from the Bible,
there won't be any New Testament reading as such.

Silence—5 seconds

Call to Worship

Leader: We have come together to worship God:
to Mount Zion, the heavenly Jerusalem,
to the city of the living God;
to thousands upon thousands of angels in joyful assembly,
to the church of the firstborn, whose names are written in heaven;
to God, the judge of all;
to the spirits of the righteous made perfect;
to Jesus, the mediator of a new covenant.

All: **So let us be thankful,**
and offer to God acceptable worship with reverence and awe.

Song Come, let us praise the Lord
(metrical version of Psalm 95, Mission Praise 92)

Old Testament Reading

Jeremiah 31.31–34

silence

Confession of Sin

Jesus is the mediator of God's new covenant.
He became like us in every respect,
so that he might be a merciful
and faithful high priest in the service of God,
to make a sacrifice of atonement for the sins of the people.
Let us draw near to God,
recalling our sins
and seeking his forgiveness.

Silence

All: **O God, our Father, whose Son Jesus Christ**
was tempted in every way as we are,
yet without sin,
we approach your throne of grace with confidence,
knowing that he understands us.
In our weakness show us your mercy,
and give us your grace to help in time of need,
for Jesus' sake. Amen.

Leader: In full assurance of faith,
with our hearts sprinkled clean from a guilty conscience,
and our bodies washed with pure water,
let us hold firm to the faith we profess,
for he who promised is faithful.

Affirmation of Faith

All: Long ago God spoke to our ancestors
in many and various ways by the prophets,
but in these last days
he has spoken to us by a Son, Jesus Christ;

Side 1: Whom he appointed heir of all things,
through whom he also created the worlds.

Side 2: He is the reflection of God's glory
and the exact imprint of God's very being,
and he sustains all things by his powerful word.

 1: When he had made purification for our sins,
he sat down at the right hand of the Majesty on high,

 2: So he became as much superior to the angels
as the name he has inherited is more excellent than theirs.

 1: Though for a little while he was made lower than the angels,
now we see Jesus crowned with glory and honour
because of the suffering of death,
so that by the grace of God he might taste death for everyone.

 2: Though he was a Son,
he learned obedience through what he suffered;
and having been made perfect,
he became the source of eternal salvation for all who obey him.

 1: Jesus, the apostle and high priest of our confession,
was faithful to the one who appointed him.

 2: He holds his priesthood permanently,
because he continues for ever.

1: Consequently he is able for all time
to save completely those who come to God through him,
since he always lives to intercede for them.

2: Such a high priest meets our need—
one who is holy, blameless, pure, set apart from sinners,
exalted above the heavens.

1: He entered once for all into the Holy Place,
not with the blood of goats and bulls,
but with his own blood,
offering himself without blemish through the eternal Spirit,
thus obtaining eternal redemption.

2: Having been offered once to bear the sins of many,
Christ will appear a second time,
not to deal with sin,
but to save those who are eagerly waiting for him.

All: **So let us fix our eyes on Jesus,**
the pioneer and perfecter of our faith,
who for the joy set before him
endured the cross,
scorning its shame,
and sat down at the right hand of the throne of God.
Amen.

Prayers

Leader: Consider him:
Jesus Christ, the same yesterday and today and for ever.
The one who sanctifies
and those who are sanctified
all have one Father.
So let us pray together the Lord's Prayer...

Leader: And let us join in this prayer for God's help

All: **Almighty God,**
by whose grace alone we are accepted
and called to your service:
strengthen us by your Holy Spirit
and make us worthy of our calling;
through Jesus Christ our Lord.
Amen.

Other prayers may be said.

All: **May the God of peace,**
who brought back from the dead our Lord Jesus,
the great shepherd of the sheep,
by the blood of the eternal covenant,
make us complete in everything good
so that we may do his will,
working in us what is pleasing in his sight,
through Jesus Christ,
to whom be glory for ever and ever.
Amen.

Song   Jesus is King and we will extol him
(Mission Praise 366, changed into first person plural)

Conclusion

These five sample liturgies should not be the last word.

May they enthuse you to look on the Bible as a source book for your worship—try and see what you can do!

These five texts can be downloaded from the Grove Books website **http://www.grovebooks.co.uk**. Further texts sent to the author, care of Grove Books, may also be made available there.

Notes

1 *Common Worship—Services and Prayers for the Church of England*, main volume p 291.

2 Main volume p 147; and there are other Scripture-based affirmations from Corinthians, Ephesians and Revelation.

3 FL Cross, *1 Peter—A Paschal Liturgy* (London: Mowbray, 1954), H Windisch and H Preisker, *Die katholischen Briefe* (Tübingen: JCB Mohr, 1951).

4 Alan Garrow, *Revelation* (London: Routledge, 1997).

5 Private communication, 2002.

6 Michael Perry, *Dramatised Bible* (London: Marshall Pickering/Bible Society, 1989).

7 A recent example is James Chatham, *Enacting the word* (Louisville/London: Westminster John Knox Press, 2002).

8 Good examples can be found in *Church Family Worship* (London: Hodders, 1986), Michael Perry, *Bible Praying* (London: HarperCollins, 1992) and *New Patterns for Worship* (London: Church House Publishing, 2002).

9 See for example W Wink, *Transforming Bible Study* (London: SCM, 1981).

10 Philip Newell, *An Earthful of Glory* (London: SPCK, 1996).

11 In the Acts 8 example in this booklet, verses from Isaiah are used—the book that the Ethiopian was reading.

12 For example in the Church of England, does your service contain all the elements required for *A Service of the Word* (see *Common Worship* main volume pp 24–27)?

13 I would be delighted to hear of your successes—do write or email me c/o Grove Books.

14 The word *labyrinth* has been used to describe these journeys. Two cautions though: this word *can* refer to a complex maze, with multiple branches; and in recent years Youth For Christ has offered a touring, high-tech experience with a similar structure called *The Labyrinth*.

15 St Mary's Ealing, 1986: author's reminiscence.

16 Thanks to Carolyn Headley (Tutor in Spirituality and Liturgy at Wycliffe Hall, Oxford) for supplying this text, which has been abbreviated.

17 Contributed by Colin Buchanan (Bishop of Woolwich), who kindly accepted some modifications by the author.

18 Kindly contributed by Colin Buchanan.

19 Thanks to Jenny Petersen (Chaplain of Queen Mary and Westfield College, London) for this liturgy. If this text is reproduced for worship use, it should bear the NRSV copyright notice from page 2 of this booklet.